GALVESTON

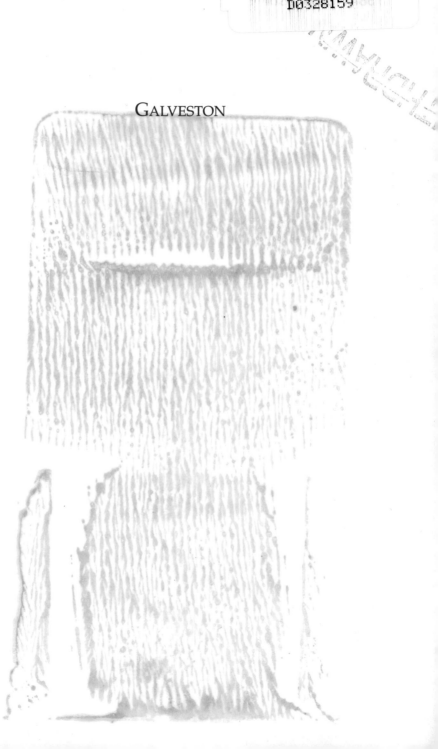

"Galvie Stone" was Galveston's first pinup girl. The Chamber of Commerce purchased the painting from New York illustrator Clarence F. Underwood in the early
twentieth century and used it for advertising purposes. The picture has disappeared, and in spite of efforts by the Galveston Chamber of Commerce to locate it
in 1995, its fate remains a mystery. Here she appears in an early brochure for the
Galvez Hotel. *Courtesy the Rosenberg Library, Galveston, Texas.*

GALVESTON

A History and a Guide

By David G. McComb

TEXAS STATE
HISTORICAL ASSOCIATION

Library of Congress Cataloging-in-Publication Data

McComb, David G.
  Galveston : a history and a guide/by David G. McComb.
    p. cm. - - (Fred Rider Cotten popular history series ; no. 15)
  Includes bibliographical references.
  ISBN 0-87611-178-9 (alk. paper)
    1. Galveston (Tex.)- -History. 2. Galveston (Tex.)- -Guidebooks. I. Title. II. Series.

  F394.G2 M364 2000
  976.4'139- -dc21

                                                          00-034342

Number fifteen in the Fred Rider Cotten Popular History Series.

Published by the Texas State Historical Association in cooperation with the Center for Studies in Texas History at the University of Texas at Austin.

Cover: The tall ship *Elissa* at Pier 22, Galveston Island, Texas. Photograph copyright 1998 by Robert Mihovil, Galveston, Texas.

CONTENTS

"Galveston, Seawall Blvd. Area 1936," shows the line of the seawall with fishing piers and bathhouses reaching into the water. Due to wave action the beaches near the wall have receded while sand has accumulated to the northeast (top of photo) where Stewart Beach is located. The large building near the center of the photograph, the Buccaneer Hotel, was torn down in the 1990s. *Photograph courtesy Verkin Photo Company Collection, Center for American History, University of Texas at Austin, CN 10511.*

INTRODUCTION

WHEN YOU TRAVEL SOUTH the fifty miles from Houston along Interstate 45 to the coast the terrain creates a gradually growing sense of anticipation and attention. Older people hum the Jimmy Webb song "Galveston," which was popularized by Glen Campbell in the late 1960s. No one, not even a child, falls asleep on the way. Although the Gulf Freeway, as it has always been known, is now cluttered with strip development, unregulated billboards, and energetic towns elbowing for room, the character of the coastal plain gradually asserts itself. The land becomes unrelentingly flat, the small live oaks and cedars give way to salt marshes, and the air becomes heavy with humidity. At the edge of the mainland the freeway becomes a causeway, and with the leap of a high bridge over a small-boat channel the speeding traveler catches a quick glimpse of private fishing boats, small sailboats, and the glittering water that promises the Gulf of Mexico. Abruptly the interstate ends and funnels into Broadway, a palm-lined main street that leads tourists across the island directly to the sands of Stewart Beach, the oldest municipal beach in Texas. It is on this transit across the island that modern, high-speed voyagers recognize that they are in a different place—a place with an exotic past, a place unique in the history of Texas, a place that excites the senses, a place that rewards unhurried contemplation.

The history of Galveston divides into three parts. The first involves the establishment of a port and its importance as a gateway for commerce and people. This era ends with an exclamation point, the Great Galveston Storm of 1900, the deadliest natural disaster in the history of the United States. The second part features the devolution of Galveston into a sin city based upon an illegal and immoral triad of drinking, gambling, and prostitution. It is a rousing time of gangland killings, big band entertainment, and mafia-like control that ends at mid-century with hammering raids from the Texas Rangers and court prosecutions. The third portion of Galveston history runs to the present time, and is a story of peaceful conversion into a primary tourist location for the recreation of families. This part of the Galveston tale involves a determined restoration of graceful nineteenth-century homes, a business section reclaimed from the 1880s, and the reconstruction of a "tall ship for Texas," the *Elissa*.

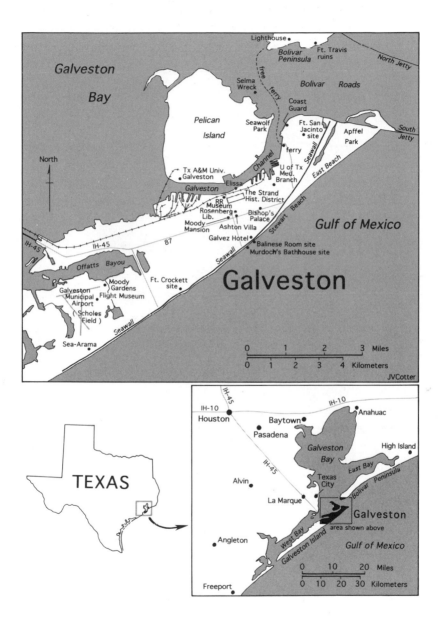

Because of Galveston's importance for commerce in Texas in the 1880s, its main business street, the Strand, was known as the "Wall Street of the South." This scene looks east from Twenty-second Street in 1894. On the right of the picture is the First National Bank Building, built in 1878 with a cast-iron front. It is now the Galveston Arts Center. *Photograph courtesy the Rosenberg Library, Galveston, Texas.*

1.
THE PORT CITY

THE TOWN BEGAN ON APRIL 20, 1838, with the first sale of city lots by the Galveston City Company. Michel B. Menard (1805–1856), a French Canadian who had worked at the Indian trade and for Texas independence, and a group of nine other associates purchased 4,605 acres at the eastern end of Galveston Island from the newly formed Republic of Texas. It was a deal in which no money exchanged hands and was based upon the future sale of the lots.[1] It was this group who firmly used the name "Galveston" for the city and island, although the name refers to Count Bernardo de Galvez, the viceroy of Mexico who ordered a mapping of the coastline in 1785. The purchase took over the best natural harbor along the Texas coast, reputedly the best sailor's shelter between New Orleans and Veracruz. Water currents in Galveston Bay had scooped out the sand to form the harbor on the leeward, or mainland, side of Galveston Island. It was deep enough to allow the sailing vessels of the time to anchor close to land and provide some protection from the periodic storms of the Gulf.

Galveston Island was a part of a curving chain of sand barrier islands some two miles off the Texas coast. They were shaped by soil washed down the rivers, carried by littoral currents, and deposited by wave action. Galveston Island, typical of the group, varied in width from one and a half miles to three miles and stretched twenty-seven miles long. In depth it was mainly sand—gray, brownish-gray, and pale yellow sand. In 1891 workers drilling for fresh water brought up in their bit various samples of sand, clay, shell, fragments of wood, and sandstone.[2] There was no bedrock; there was no potable water. So, older island dwellers caught rainwater and planted salt-resistant oleanders; modern inhabitants imported both water and topsoil.

On the mainland side, the island had a ragged shoreline of shallow salt marsh, reeds, and mudflats good for ducks and herons. On the Gulf side there was a long, even expanse of hard-packed, beige sand—the color of light brown sugar—that from the start of Anglo settlement provided the best beach in Texas for recreation. Francis C. Sheridan, an Irishman in the British Diplomatic Service who otherwise found the town "singularly dreary" in 1839–1840, wrote that the beach had the "whitest, firmest, & most beautiful sand I ever saw."[3] At a time of unpaved, stumpy, and rutted dirt roads it was pure pleasure to drive a light buggy with a spirited horse over the tight-packed sand bordering the surf amid the whirling cries of gulls and the low rumble of waves.[4] The beach proved to be the most important and enduring recreational asset for the city.

Wildlife abounded. In the marshes of the bay shores flourished frogs, snakes, bees, butterflies, herons, blackbirds, mice, ducks, shellfish, and an occasional alligator. Rattlesnakes, rabbits, and deer lived in the dunes of the island, and along the Gulf all sorts of sea birds scavenged for a living. There were, for example, some fifty-three varieties of seagulls—the most common was the laughing gull, identified by its dark red legs and raucous laugh. Galveston is in the midst of the central flyway for birds of the United States, and continues to attract bird-watchers for the spring and fall migrations. In the surrounding waters were shrimp, flounder, red snapper, Spanish mackerel, sheepshead, croakers, and speckled trout. There were also some sharks, and the occasional whale or sea turtle. Silver king tarpon could be caught from piers and jetties, but numbers declined after 1965, either due to pollution or overfishing. The numbers of tarpon have recently increased thanks to conservation measures.[5] Galveston Island, thus, was an interesting place to visit from the very beginning.

The earliest human visitors were Karankawa Indians on hunting expeditions who waded or poled their way to the island in crude dugout logs. The men wore no clothing and pierced their nipples and lower lips with large pieces of cane. The women covered themselves with Spanish moss or deerskin. The Karankawas carved blue, curved tattoos on their faces, and smeared their bodies with smelly shark or alligator oil to repel mosquitoes. They spent their time hunting, fishing, and gathering seasonal roots, nuts, berries, and shellfish. They never learned the arts of metallurgy or agriculture. The Karankawas treated their children with kindness, celebrated marriage and death with elaborate rituals, and, at least at first, gave sympathy and aid to Europeans.[6]

Insight into the Karankawas' lives came through the report of Álvar Núñez Cabeza de Vaca (1490?–1556?), a durable Spanish explorer who was shipwrecked on the beach in November 1528. He was the second in command of the doomed *entrada* of Pánfilo de Narváez, which sought gold and glory in Florida, but found only hostile Indians and death. After being abandoned by their transport ships on the Gulf Coast of Florida, Narváez and his four hundred men built barges in order to float along the shore to Mexico. Most perished on the way, including Narváez, but some eighty to ninety washed up on the shores of Galveston Island or nearby Follets Island. Of these, only four survived, and one of them, Cabeza de Vaca, wrote about the adventure.[7]

Karankawa Indians greeted the stranded Spaniards and traded food for bells and beads. De Vaca's group tried to resume their voyage, stored their clothing and equipment on their barge, pushed it into the surf, and lost everything when the crude vessel turned over one hundred yards from shore. The dripping, naked men struggled back through the chilling wind and surf to the cold sand. The observing Indians understood their plight, and as was their custom, sat down to cry in sympathy for thirty minutes. Then the Karankawas built a series of warming fires and relayed the men back to their camp, where they treated them to food, shelter, and an all-night dance.

Exposure, malnutrition, and dysentery, however, soon began to kill both Spaniards and natives. Shocked Karankawas, moreover,

From 1814 to 1821 Jean Laffite, the "Pirate of the Gulf" used the natural harbor on Galveston Island as a base. Forced to evacuate by the United States Navy, Laffite left the island on his ship, the *Pride*, and disappeared into the mists of legend and rumor. *Courtesy the Rosenberg Library, Galveston, Texas.*

discovered that a small group of isolated Spaniards had eaten their own fellows in order to survive. All of this turned the Indians against the Europeans and the remaining survivors, including Cabeza de Vaca, were enslaved. After six years Cabeza de Vaca and three others escaped and walked to safety in Mexico.[8] The subsequent report of Cabeza de Vaca to the Spanish authorities provided the first written description of southwestern America.

Galveston Island where Cabeza de Vaca came ashore was only eight to nine feet above sea level at the highest, and infested with rattlesnakes. It was too exposed, barren, and uncomfortable to support a permanent Indian camp. The first sustained settlement came much later with the pirates of the early nineteenth century. During the first quarter of the century when revolutions crumbled the Spanish New World Empire, a priest, Don José Manuel de Herrera, who represented the rebels of Mexico, appointed Louis Michel Aury, a French privateer, commodore of the Mexican

Navy. Aury raided Spanish vessels and set up a ragtag base at the natural harbor on Galveston Island. He marketed his contraband through the port of New Orleans. After transporting a rebel army to the Spanish town of Soto La Marina in April 1817, however, Aury met a surprise when he returned to his headquarters. Jean Laffite, a buccaneer from New Orleans, had taken over and Aury had to move on to Florida.

Laffite (1780?–1825?) was a double agent—Mexico and Spain— who preyed on Spanish shipping for his own profit. He called his community of a thousand outlaws at Galveston, "Campechy on Snake Island," and served as a broker for the freebooters who brought their loot to him. In exchange for food, gunpowder, and shot, Laffite took the stolen jewelry, silks, laces, and slaves by mule train to the backdoor bayous of New Orleans for illegal sale into the United States. Although operating outside the border of the United States, Laffite was a nuisance, and a U.S. Navy warship politely invited him to leave. Consequently, in 1821 Laffite burned Campechy; boarded his privateer, *Pride*, with his gorgeous, black-eyed, quadroon mistress; sailed into the Caribbean; and disappeared forever into the mists of history.[9] He left behind nothing but a lurid memory and rumors of buried treasure.

Mexico, having attained independence from Spain in 1821, briefly established and then abandoned a customhouse at the harbor. During the Texas Revolution in 1836 the island and the harbor served as a last point of refuge for the retreating Texas government. After victory at San Jacinto in April, however, the government moved to Velasco, a small coastal settlement near the mouth of the Brazos River, and the future of Galveston Island became uncertain. It was at this point, however, that Michel Menard and his associates purchased the land on the eastern tip.

Levi Jones (1792–1878), one of the partners, became the general agent for land sales, and hired John D. Groesbeck (1816–1856) to survey and subdivide the property. He laid out the town in gridiron fashion, with the avenues running parallel to the harbor labeled in alphabetical order. Streets crossed the avenues at right angles, and Groesbeck numbered them in sequence. In time, some of the numbers and letters changed—Avenue B became the

THEN AND NOW
THE BOLIVAR FERRY

The free automotive ferry between the tip of Bolivar Peninsula and Galveston Island that connects Highway 87 is one of the unadvertised pleasures maintained by the Texas Department of Transportation. Travelers to the peninsula can visit the ruins of Fort Travis (1898–1943), which was built for harbor defense. It was on this same site that Jane Long, the "Mother of Texas," gave birth to the first Anglo child in Texas in 1821. Nearby is the north jetty used to focus the tidal currents to scour the Galveston Bay channel clear of sandbars. Also dominant on the flat terrain is the iron Bolivar lighthouse, which operated from 1872 to 1933. It holds a place in history as a refuge during hurricanes and as a practice target for undisciplined coastal gunners in World War I. It is now privately owned.

Toward Galveston the traveler on the ferry can see the buildings of the city, the Port of Galveston, the abandoned emigration station, and the partly sunken concrete wreck *Selma*, built for World War I. Living mainly on fish that he caught, "Frenchy" LaBlanc, a recluse, used the grounded vessel as a home shortly after World War II. The three-mile ferry trip with its boat whistles, swirling seagulls, and movement over water sets a mood of sea and land. It serves as the best introduction for visitors to Galveston.

"Strand," Avenue E became "Postoffice," and Avenue J became "Broadway." In 1838 the Galveston City Company sold lots and by the end of the year it had disposed of seven hundred sites for an average price of four hundred dollars each. There were more than one hundred structures and sixty families living there when the Texas Congress granted incorporation in 1839. Adult, white, male property owners could vote and they elected John M. Allen (?–1847), a hero of the Battle of San Jacinto, as the first mayor.[10]

The town attracted a mixed group of citizens—American, English, German, Dutch, Italian, Mexican, and African. The men wore boots, trousers, frock coats made from blankets, and carried pistols and Bowie knives. Business took place in bars where there was not only the convenience of liquor, but also a spitting box for those chewing tobacco. "High & low, rich & poor, young & old chew, chew, chew & spit, spit, spit all the blessed day & most of the night," complained Sheridan, the British diplomat.[11] Merchants, known as factors, such as Thomas F. McKinney (1801-1873) and Samuel May Williams (1795-1858) set up warehouses and began to trade in the produce of coastal Texas. Cotton, hides, sugar, molasses, honey, cattle, and pecans were sent to New Orleans, New York, and Great Britain while manufactured items such as cloth, boots, coffee, books, iron tools, gunpowder, bullets, and guns traveled inland to supply the needs of farmers and plantation owners.

The harbor at Galveston was a pivotal point of Texas trade. It was deep enough for the blue water sailing ships of the time. Cargo and travelers, however, had to be transferred to a different mode of transport to reach the interior of Texas. Deep water ships could not maneuver in shallow Galveston Bay, and the plantations lay inland beyond the marshy salt flats of the coast. So, at Galveston stevedores moved the cargoes from the holds of the large vessels to the decks of small, shallow-draft steamboats. The steamboats, spouting sparks and smoke from their funnels, sailed through Galveston Bay, which was seven to eight feet deep, and up the tortuous Buffalo Bayou to Houston, which was a small inland trading town at that time.

At Houston dock workers moved the shipping items to ox wagons for transport over crude roads to the farms and plantations of the hinterland. When cotton and other country products were ready after harvest, the transportation system reversed itself to carry the materials to Galveston. The rhythm of commerce, therefore, was that of crops and harvests, but storage warehouses, docks, and factors flourished in the towns to facilitate the trade. During growing season or wintertime, the towns languished and awaited the bounty of nature. But, towns were vital to the economy of nineteenth-century Texas, and they were essential links in the transportation network.[12]

Galveston grew to be the most important city in Texas in the 1870s and 1880s when its population, reaching 22,000, was the largest Texas city. Its strength lay in its natural harbor and commerce, which formed a near monopoly of trade along the Texas coast. Outsiders complained that the Galveston Wharf Company, which had controlled the docks since before the Civil War, was greedy, and called it the "Octopus of the Gulf." This monopoly crumbled, however, with the advent of new technologies—railroads and harbor dredging.[13]

Harvest season, in the wet fall of the year, was when heavy ox wagons carried cotton bales to Houston over muddy roads in what was often an agonizing journey. When the wagons sank to their axles in mud holes, they had to be unloaded. The teamsters then pried the wagon from the muck, reloaded, and traveled a bit farther until it sank again. Progress was so slow that at times the wagoneers could look back down their path at night and see where they had camped the day before. Railway technology, imported from the eastern United States, solved the problem of impassable roads by lifting travelers out of the mud. It was no surprise that Houston became the the railroad center of the state before the Civil War with rails reaching out in all directions as far as a hundred miles. The years between the end of the war and the end of the nineteenth century were when the railroads formed spiderwebs of connections across the state, not only to the Galveston-Houston trade corridor, but also to the northeast and east, to Chicago, St. Louis, and New Orleans. Texas farmers, plantation owners, and ranchers, consequently, were no longer dependent upon muddy roads, or for that matter, the natural port at Galveston Island.

Galveston merchants, among the richest in the state, did not hesitate to join the railroad builders. A cannon's boom announced the first train of the Galveston, Houston and Henderson (GH&H), which reached the island over a two-mile trestle in 1860. This was a trunk line between Houston and Galveston designed to carry cotton from the warehouses of the Bayou City to the docks at Galveston harbor. The small Galveston Bay steamboats were no longer needed and that colorful industry slowly languished and died. Following the Civil War the transcontinental railroads moving east and west drained the port's commerce, but it remained important for cotton shipments to Europe.[14]

Galveston cotton merchants led in efforts to improve the harbor as ships became larger and transport technology changed. The

THEN AND NOW

APFFEL PARK AND THE SOUTH JETTY

Ships moving through the Galveston Bay channel can be seen from the northern end of the seawall. The section of the seawall that connects to the south jetty was built by the United States government in 1921 to protect Fort San Jacinto. The south jetty, like the north jetty across the channel on the Bolivar Peninsula, has served successfully for a century to reduce the channel's sandbars by focusing the tidal currents of the bay to scour the bottom clear of sediment. The littoral current moving parallel to the shoreline, in turn, has deposited the sand to create the broad expanse of Apffel Park. Known in the 1980s for its rowdy crowds, it is now noted for its young adult concerts and as the site of the annual American Institute of Architects sandcastle contests in early June. It is the only Galveston beach where cars are allowed to drive up to the water's edge.

tidal bore that had scooped out the harbor and provided a forty-foot-deep channel between the tip of Galveston Island and the Bolivar Peninsula to the northeast also created sandbars that became particularly difficult to cross in the late 1860s. Amid the increasing frustration, the idea emerged to use jetties to direct the flow of the tidal current to scour the channel free of sandbars, and to persuade the federal government to pay for it. Led by Col. William L. Moody (1828–1920), a cotton factor, the important island businessmen formed a Deep Water Committee to seek out the best solution and to lobby Congress. It took time, but in 1890 a Galveston Harbor Bill for jetties passed. The whistles of the city—on trains, steamships, and factories—blasted the air for thirty minutes in celebration.

The U.S. Army Corps of Engineers built two rail trestles over the water reaching five miles into the Gulf to construct a north jetty from Bolivar, and a south jetty from Galveston Island. They dumped five-ton blocks of sandstone from rail cars into the water to build a wall, and when it reached the surface, they capped it with ten-ton, hard granite blocks that reached five feet above the water. The project cost $8,700,000, but it successfully directed the

Galveston was the leading cotton shipping port in the United States in 1900. Here dock workers move cotton bales onto an ocean-going vessel. *Photograph courtesy the Rosenberg Library, Galveston, Texas.*

current. In October 1896 the British steamer *Algoa*, the largest cargo ship in the world, drawing twenty-one feet of water, tied up at the Galveston docks. Within a few years Galveston exports had doubled and by the end of the century the city was the leading cotton export harbor in the nation.[15] It was a triumph of engineering and urban determination, but there were other problems for the city.

Harbor improvement and dredging techniques could be used to help other places as well. It was no longer necessary to possess a natural harbor. In 1896 Congress agreed to dredge a ship channel through Galveston Bay and Buffalo Bayou to Houston. The Houston Ship Channel opened in 1914, and Houston, once Galveston's junior partner, grew to become one of the top three ports in the nation. Port Arthur opened in 1899; Texas City, across the trestle from Galveston, dredged a harbor in 1904; Beaumont developed a port in 1908. By the end of the twentieth century Galveston ranked only sixth in tonnage handled by various Texas ports.[16]

Although it slipped economically due to railroads, harbor technology, and the pattern of Texas growth, Galveston possessed a cultural and social life that made it unmistakably different, a place unlike the rest of Texas. Before the Civil War Galveston offered a concentration of entertainment and recreation that could not be found in the countryside. There were saloons with juleps and cobblers, hunting, fishing, buggy rides on the beach, nude swimming in the surf, bookstores, lectures, formal debates, theatre performances, and the long-lasting Galveston Artillery Company that organized in 1840 for home protection, parades, and fancy dress balls.[17] Galveston Island was the place to go for a good time. In 1838 the prissy Methodist missionary Littleton Fowler took a vacation trip to Galveston with Sam Houston and members of the Texas Congress. They traveled by steamboat down Buffalo Bayou from Houston, then the seat of government. Most of the men became drunk, stripped to their underwear, and told loud profane stories. Minister Fowler was so shocked that when he returned home he took to his bed and almost died, so he said, because the roisterous vacation caused the return of an earlier illness.[18]

At Galveston there was also the entertainment of the curious genius of Gail Borden (1801–1874), who was a member of the first city government and an agent for the Galveston City Company. He was an oddball character and inventor who had patented a meat biscuit—condensed boiled meat mixed with flour—that could be eaten by travelers and soldiers as rations. The problem with the meat biscuit (and the reason that it failed) was that it tasted terrible. Borden also built a "terraqueous machine" that could roll down the beach with a sail, and then take to the water where the wind power turned a screw for propulsion. His maiden voyage was a social disaster when his frightened passengers all rushed to one side and dumped everyone into the surf. Later, however, after leaving Galveston, Borden learned how to condense milk, made a great success with it during the Civil War, and established a company that endures to the present time.[19]

The war brought a Union naval blockade that halted the port's commerce. Confederate soldiers occupied the town; blockade runners with small boats and steamers used the harbor; and townspeople fled inland to avoid deprivation and the bombardment by Federal ships. Texas and Galveston were far removed from the decisive theaters of war, but did experience an interesting fight called the Battle of Galveston. In order to reduce the cost of maintaining the United States blockade along the long Texas coastline, Rear Adm. David G. Farragut decided to send troops to occupy the major ports. At Galveston, Comdr. W. B. Renshaw sailed into the harbor, demanded surrender, and the city gave up. Renshaw did not have enough personnel to occupy the entire island, and so he landed soldiers who raised the United States flag over the customhouse during the daytime and retreated to Kuhn's Wharf at night.

Confederate Gen. John B. Magruder (1807–1871) decided to retake Galveston and ordered a combined sea and land attack. He sent two small steamers that had been converted to gunboats and armored with cotton bales down Buffalo Bayou to attack the six Federal ships in the harbor while Confederate soldiers crossed the railroad bridge into the city. The fighting began at 5:00 a.m. on January 1, 1863, with the Confederate soldiers assaulting the barricaded Yankee troops on the wharf. The cotton clads attacked the highly prized northern ship *Harriet Lane*, but the *Lane* sank one of the oncoming Rebel boats. The other cotton clad, however, rammed the *Lane* and the Confederates scrambled on board. The Confederates won the hand-to-hand combat and captured the *Harriet Lane*, which turned out to be the main trophy of the battle. Renshaw died while trying to blow up one of his ships that had gone aground, and the rest of the Union fleet fled all the way to New Orleans. The Federal soldiers on shore had no choice but to surrender. Magruder thus retook the city and captured some three to four hundred prisoners.[20]

Galveston remained in Confederate hands until the end of the war when Magruder surrendered to the captain of the blockading squadron. Northern occupation troops arrived, and Gen. Gordon Granger, the Federal officer in charge, pronounced an emancipation

"Attack of the rebels upon our gun-boat flotilla at Galveston, Texas, January 1, 1863." From *Harper's Weekly*, January 31, 1863. *Courtesy Prints and Photographs Collection, Center for American History, University of Texas at Austin, CN 06262.*

proclamation for Texas slaves on June 19, 1865. Ever since that moment, June 19, otherwise known as "Juneteenth Day," became a holiday for black citizens of Texas and the Southwest.

The city quickly recovered from the war as former townspeople returned, and some three thousand Yankee soldiers disembarked to enforce Reconstruction policies. Trains began to run three times a day back and forth to Houston, river steamers began to arrive with cotton, and there arose a high demand for lumber, nails, and cement as the town rebuilt. With so many unacclimatized people on the island, however, yellow fever struck like a punishing angel. This epidemic virus, spread through mosquito bites, killed with a twenty to twenty-five percent mortality rate of those infected. At the time no one understood the cause of the disease, but it was known to affect Gulf Coast ports in summer months until the first hard frost (which

"Old Red," designed by famed Galveston architect Nicholas J. Clayton, in 1890 was the first building on the campus of the University of Texas Medical Center. *Photograph by David G. McComb.*

killed the mosquitoes). Galveston suffered epidemics in 1839, 1844, 1847, 1853, 1854, 1858, 1859, 1864, 1867, 1870, and 1873. States finally controlled yellow fever through the quarantine of infected places, and later, when the etiology was understood, through mosquito control. In Galveston in 1867 people died at a rate of twenty per day with the church bells tolling death knells almost without stop.[21]

It was disease like yellow fever, ironically, that brought the city its most prestigious institution, the University of Texas Medical Branch. With the formation of the University of Texas in 1881 the people of Texas voted to place the medical school in Galveston, persuaded in part by the argument that the port had the greatest number of maladies for students to study. The city donated a block of land for the facility and John Sealy (1822–1884), a wealthy merchant, gave $50,000 for a teaching hospital. Nicholas J. Clayton (1840–1916), a local architect, designed

"Old Red," which was the first building on the campus, and the Sealy family continued to pay expenses and add new buildings to insure the success of the school.[22]

Although Galveston had slipped in population numbers and economic importance compared to other Texas cities at the dawn of the twentieth century, it was still a most attractive place. Clayton built elegant Victorian homes, the city developed a fresh water supply by pumping water through pipes from the mainland, the cotton business flourished, the medical school provided an intellectual lift, and bathhouses on the beach heralded a developing recreation industry. There was a growing military presence, too, as the United States government began the construction of Fort Crockett in 1897 on the Gulf shore for the training of coastal artillerymen. All seemed well. Then disaster struck Galveston—the worst natural catastrophe in terms of death in all of American history.

During the nineteenth century hurricanes had hit Galveston Island at least eleven times. In 1837, for instance, while Texans were using the island as a base, a storm floated vessels over the land and left eight of them stranded. Rain from the storms periodically flooded the city, and a rival port down the coast, Indianola, had been twice destroyed by hurricanes. Galvestonians should have known better, but when the skies were bright blue and the breeze was warm, it was hard to think about anything dire. Moreover, people accepted the comforting theory of Matthew F. Maury, a national marine authority, who said that Galveston was located in a "cove of safety," protected by shallow water and sandbars.[23]

Isaac M. Cline, the resident climatologist, became suspicious in early September 1900 when he noticed long swells breaking on the Gulf shore and a tide above normal. The weather service had informed him by telegraph of a storm in the Gulf, and as the barometer slowly dropped, Cline hitched up a horse and buggy to warn people away from the beach. Hurricane flags—two red squares with black squares in the center—were sent whipping in the growing wind up the flagpoles in town. No one, not even Cline, guessed how bad it was going to be.[24]

Urban rubble piled up by the hurricane of 1900 contained household items, structural materials, and bodies. *Photograph courtesy the Rosenberg Library, Galveston, Texas.*

On Saturday evening, September 8, 1900, the hurricane swept in from the Gulf with gusts of 120 miles per hour and a storm surge of fourteen and a half feet. The wind blew against the tide, which meant that bay water coursed in from the north and storm water from the south. It flooded the city and destroyed about six blocks of buildings on the Gulf side. The debris churning in the water battered standing houses until they collapsed while gusts of wind sent pieces of slate roof slicing through the air with deadly force. Piles of urban remains ten to twenty feet high containing wood, metal, glass, furniture, household items of all sorts, and bodies formed a crude breakwater through the town. About six thousand people of Galveston died in this night of terror.

On Sunday morning the sun rose out of a calm sea into a clear sky while the dazed survivors, cut off from the mainland, emerged from the wet wreckage to face the horror around them. Rescue,

The 1900 hurricane destroyed one-third of the city and killed an estimated six thousand people. This is the remainder of the Sacred Heart Catholic Church. *Photograph courtesy the Rosenberg Library, Galveston, Texas.*

relief, and recovery were organized by Mayor Walter C. Jones, who appointed a Central Relief Committee of leading citizens. They were assigned specific tasks such as finance, burials, relief, and hospitals. The new committee took care of the emergency while the elected council took care of political matters. The system worked

As the hurricane waters of 1900 receded the survivors gathered the bodies with makeshift stretchers for identification and disposal. *Photograph courtesy the Rosenberg Library, Galveston, Texas.*

well since in such emergencies most people cooperate for the welfare of others. Reports of looting were largely unsubstantiated.

Aid poured in from the outside. The Texas militia arrived and Jones turned police duties over to the soldiers on September 13. Clara Barton and the Red Cross showed up on September 17, after immediate recovery was well under way. Everyone worked to clear the debris and dispose of bodies. At first there was an attempt to bury people at sea, but the bloated corpses drifted back to the beach. The ground was too saturated for burials on land, and so the practical solution was to burn the bodies on the piles of debris. This grisly task continued into November.

Meanwhile, in the first week workers restored telephone, telegraph, and water lines. The first train arrived over the repaired trestle on September 22, the same day that martial law was revoked. After three weeks the Houston relief groups went home,

Hurricane victims of 1900 were lined up in a warehouse for identification and disposal. Since the ground was saturated with water, most bodies were cremated. *Photograph courtesy the Rosenberg Library, Galveston, Texas.*

the electric trolley began to operate, freight began moving through the harbor, and the saloons reopened. On October 14, one of Galveston's largest shipments of cotton, 30,300 bales, cleared the port. The Central Relief Committee, boosted by $1,250,000 in donations from around the world, continued to operate its commissary until the second week in February, and thus in six months time Galveston had recovered to the point that no one needed welfare, commerce had revived, and the population could begin to think about its future.[25]

The Galvez Hotel opened in 1911, at a time when sand remained in front of the sea-wall and early automobiles could drive along the beach. The construction of the Galvez Hotel marks a recognition by city business leaders about the importance of tourism. *Photograph courtesy the Rosenberg Library, Galveston, Texas.*

2.
THE SIN CITY

THE OLD DEEP WATER COMMITTEE (DWC), which had formed earlier to promote the building of the jetties, had continued to function as an ad hoc group for the promotion of the city. It was an organization of wealthy businessmen who had a stake in the welfare of Galveston. Within days of the hurricane R. Waverly Smith, Walter Gresham, and Farrell D. Minor, who were members of the committee, began to work on a new form of government that the businessmen could control. With the Central Relief Committee as a model their plan called for the governor of the state to appoint a mayor and four commissioners. Each commissioner would take on a specific task—police and fire, waterworks and sewers, streets and public improvements, and finance and revenue. The plan was undemocratic since citizens would have no opportunity to vote for city officials. With no referendum of the residents the DWC appealed directly to the state legislature for a charter change. The legislature complied, but inserted a democratic element by insisting that the people elect two of the commissioners. The commission government thus took over in Galveston one year after the great hurricane.[26]

Eventually, all commissioners became subject to election, and the so-called commission plan of city government became a nationally

Built after the great storm in the early twentieth century, the seawall protected Galveston from future storms. Engineers designed it with interlocking concrete sections seventeen feet high. *Photograph courtesy the Rosenberg Library, Galveston, Texas.*

popular form of urban government in the first two decades of the twentieth century. The plan, however, contained an inherent flaw, because the commissioners who possessed both legislative and executive authority within their defined areas often refused to cooperate with their colleagues. For efficiency, many cities that had adopted the commission form turned to a city-manager format. Galveston, too, eventually changed to that format in 1961.

One of the first actions of the new government was to take steps to protect the city from future hurricanes. It might have been that the people would simply abandon the city site as had been done in Indianola, but there was a fierce desire by citizens to remain. It was known as the "Galveston Spirit," actually a common phenomenon of people in disaster to reassert themselves and rebuild. As Maj. Robert Lowe, manager of the Galveston *Daily News*, responded to a suggestion by a Dallas journalist to print the paper in Houston, "You would, would you? Well, I won't," he shouted. "You never lived here. You don't know—and you would ask me to desert? No, no, no! This paper lives or dies with this town. We'll

THEN AND NOW

SEAWALL BOULEVARD AND TWENTY-FIRST STREET

At this point on the seawall can be seen the Galvez Hotel, which was constructed in 1911 for the tourist industry. Sam Maceo, the gangster chieftain, lived in a suite in the hotel and hosted a second wedding ceremony for his friend bandleader Phil Harris and singer Alice Faye. The mayor and the police chief were among the reception guests. The hotel, although remodeled many times, reflects its history in its basic design and with historic photographs on its walls. Across the street on a closed pier is the Maceos' abandoned Balinese Room, once the most famous nightclub on the Texas coast.

As you move southward along the seawall to Twenty-third Street (Tremont Street) the stumps of pilings on the beach mark the location of Murdoch's Bathhouse, which served 125,000 swimmers with dressing rooms and bathing suits in 1929. A hurricane destroyed it in 1961, and a souvenir shop has taken its place. At this busy intersection—the first Galveston traffic signals appeared here in 1924—are two large weathered stone monuments honoring the completion of the city seawall segment in 1904. The structure of the seawall is easily seen—five feet across the top, concrete concave face, riprap at the base, and tongue-in-groove seams that locked the huge segments of the wall together. J. M. O'Rourke, one of the principal contractors, when asked to speak at the seawall dedication ceremony said simply, "I will not say anything for the wall, for if it ever has an opportunity you will find it well able to talk for itself." (Galveston *Daily News*, Aug. 23, 1904).

build it again and *The News* will help."[27] The newspaper continued to print in Galveston and did not miss an issue.

The city took three steps to protect itself from the storms of the Gulf. First, the commissioners hired a panel of three engineers—Henry M. Robert, Alfred Noble, and H. C. Ripley—to design a seawall. When constructed, it was a solid barrier of reinforced concrete seventeen feet high, five feet wide at the top, fifteen feet wide at the bottom, and three miles long to shield the Gulf face of the city. It weighed 40,000 pounds per foot and presented a concave front to the sea to divert the force of angry waves upward. Loose piles of four-foot squares of granite served as riprap to protect the

Part of the program to protect Galveston from hurricanes after 1900 was to raise the ground level of the town. People jacked up their houses and pumped slurry of sand from the harbor to leave a deposit of underlying fill dirt. These before-and-after pictures illustrate the enormous amount of sand that was necessary for this monumental task. *Photographs courtesy the Rosenberg Library, Galveston, Texas.*

To provide access to the island and an escape route when hurricanes threatened, Galveston constructed an all-weather causeway to the mainland. When completed in 1912 Gov. Oscar B. Colquitt led a line of 1,500 cars to celebrate the event. *Photograph courtesy the Rosenberg Library, Galveston, Texas.*

foot of the wall from washing. With subsequent additions the wall reached 10.4 miles and became one of the outstanding marine boulevards of the nation.[28]

The second step was to raise the height of the island a greater distance above sea level. The surge of water from the Great Storm was almost twice the elevation of the land. P. C. Goedhart from Germany and Lindon W. Bates of New York formed a company to dredge watery sand from the harbor and pump it through pipes onto city lots. The water drained off, the sand remained, and the island was higher. They thus filled in behind the seawall to seventeen feet and then tapered the elevation with a two percent grade to the harbor on the bay side of the island. People jacked up houses, buildings, churches, and even gravestones as the sand poured underneath. The task took nine years but when completed the company had raised five hundred city blocks with 16,300,000 cubic yards of sand.[29]

The third step for the safety of the city was the construction of an all-weather bridge to the mainland. In moments of danger there had to be a means of escape. Earlier, only a weak causeway for wagons and several railroad trestles existed. This time the city, county, and rail companies built a combination bridge for cars, trucks, railroads, and an interurban commuter train to Houston. The engineers designed the bridge, which still stands, with twenty-eight concrete arches and a rolling lift in the center to permit the passage of small boats. It opened in 1912, but has since been replaced with modern automobile causeways in 1935 and 1956.[30] Thus, the people of Galveston, determined to remain on their vulnerable sandy isle, protected themselves with a massive seawall, grade raising, and an unbreakable link to the mainland. As with all great engineering efforts, however, the projects needed a test to prove their worth. This came in 1915.

In August a hurricane comparable to the one in 1900 roared ashore. Anxious Galvestonians huddled in buildings and nervously danced at the Galvez Hotel behind their seawall while floodwater, its force dissipated by the concave curve of the wall, seeped five to six feet deep into the downtown area. An electric interurban car, with its power cut, stalled in the middle of the causeway, but the passengers were able to walk to safety on the mainland. Every ship in the harbor suffered damage, and the three-masted schooner *Allison Doura*, caught by the storm in the Gulf south of Mobile, hurdled the seawall and smashed into splinters on the military reservation of Fort Crockett. The hurricane destroyed ninety percent of the structures outside the wall on Galveston Island and the Bolivar Peninsula, and killed 312 people.

Only eight died at Galveston, however, and in ten days the urban services of electricity, water, and streetcars were again available.[31] The seawall, grade raising, and all-weather bridge had worked and saved the city. This technology, moreover, continued

The seawall proved its worth during the hurricane of 1915 while anxious people danced through the night at the Galvez Hotel. *Photograph courtesy the Rosenberg Library, Galveston, Texas.*

to prove its worthiness through the other hurricane strikes of the twentieth century. Galveston's technological response to the disaster of 1900, an illustration of rationality and determination, represents its finest hour in history. The seawall, bridges, and grade elevation are still clearly visible; they serve as artifacts to ponder concerning the age-old struggle between humanity and nature.

Although Galveston survived as a city it did not thrive. Its treasure—tax monies and bonds—was used to pay for the defenses necessary to protect it from the storms of the Gulf. The town, moreover, missed the great Texas oil bonanza that began with the gusher at Spindletop in 1901. Fledgling oil companies chose safe inland sites for their refineries and headquarters—hence the rise of Houston—while Galveston worked out its future with the sea. Rail transportation and competing ports created by human technology deflected commerce, and after 1900 an image of lurid death in Galveston lingered in the American consciousness for a generation. The Island City, therefore, did not expand with the prosperity of Texas and the nation. Its population grew from

THEN AND NOW

THE SOUTH END OF SEAWALL BOULEVARD

The ten miles of seawall end and highway FM 3005 joins at an angle, drops off a slope, and leads on down the island to the southwest. In 1950 the blocked ramp at the end of the seawall led straight to a broad beach and visitors could drive their cars on the sand to the west end of the island. Now the ramp drops into seawater, which dramatically demonstrates the shift of the island toward the mainland. Sand barrier islands, such as Galveston Island, are always on the move. The sea, moreover, laps at the base of the wall, which illustrates the fact that the building of a seawall usually results in the loss of the beach.

The land grade behind the wall at this point has not been raised as it was in the older parts of Galveston. This segment did not receive that protection at the beginning of the century and flooding can be expected here during a hurricane. Furthermore, looking down the beach beyond the wall offers an example of what the island was like before the Great Storm of 1900. A person can see from Gulf to the inner reaches of the bay from this mere seventeen-foot elevation. People, nevertheless, have moved into vacation subdivisions down the island, and it is easy to imagine what would happen during a category five hurricane such as Camille, which struck the Louisiana-Mississippi coast in 1969 with a storm surge of twenty-two to twenty-five feet. Here lies a disaster waiting to happen.

38,000 in 1900 to 60,000 people in 1940, and then remained at about that level for the rest of the century.[32]

Galveston's destiny was to become a tourist city—a place where people go for a vacation, a place for entertainment and amusement, a place to visit but not to remain. And for Galvestonians tourism became the major source of revenue. This change occurred because of the growing popularity of the automobile and the increasing prosperity of the American people after World War I. Excursions and conventions had reached the island by railroad in the nineteenth century, but the automobile opened the world of tourism to the masses. It was symbolic when the new causeway opened in 1912 that Gov. Oscar Colquitt led a line of

The causeway of 1912 made it possible for tourists to visit by automobile. The first motels appeared along the Gulf shore in the 1920s. *Photograph courtesy the Rosenberg Library, Galveston, Texas.*

1,500 cars across the two miles of water, onto the island, and out to the Galvez Hotel for a day of speeches, fireworks, eating, and dancing. Galveston was accessible now to tourists as never before.

The town had never been without a constant stream of visitors—immigrants responding to the lure of cheap lands in Texas, Yankee soldiers disembarking to enforce the orders of Reconstruction on a conquered land, nomadic sailors striding the docks to take on cargoes of compressed cotton. As a result there was always a certain amount of licit and illicit activity to entertain the transients. It took on special emphasis during the Reconstruction period, however, when large numbers of bored, young, male soldiers occupied the city. Later, troubles along the Mexican border in 1910–1914, World War I, and World War II stationed other restless, energetic young men on the island. Galveston responded with an array of saloons, sporting houses, and bagnios that gave it the reputation of a sin city, which endured until the middle of the twentieth century.

A red-light district—centered on Postoffice Street between Twenty-sixth and Twenty-seventh—of saloons and bordellos formed in the nineteenth century. Run by enterprising madams, not by organized crime, the citizens accepted the corruption with easy tolerance. They joked that the outstretched arm of "Victory" on the pedestal of the Texas Heroes Monument of 1900 on Broadway pointed not to the distant battleground of San Jacinto as designed, but to the nearby pleasures of the district. The number of prostitutes in terms of per capita population was extraordinary—one in sixty-two in the 1930s—which created a health problem for the military encampments on the island and mainland during World War I and World War II. Outside police authorities finally padlocked the whorehouses in the late 1950s and drove them out of business.[33]

The citizens also tolerated an amazing crime family, the Maceos, who controlled illegal gambling and drinking. It was actually more than toleration. The townsfolk admired the Maceos, and were proud to live in what they called "the free state of Galveston." The stage was set by the illegality of gambling, suppressed in Texas during the 1880s, and the illegality of hard liquor, outlawed in the United States in 1919. Regardless of the laws, of course, people continued to drink and gamble, as people had done since the time of Methuselah. Galveston Island, with its long, unpatrolled beach, became the haunt of bootleggers with swift speedboats who met offshore British cargo ships, took on small loads of whiskey, and raced back to the island where they unloaded the crates along the beach, or sometimes, at private docks. The smugglers then sent their high quality whiskey over the highways on trucks to midwestern cities, or by rail hidden as shipments of scrap metal destined for Detroit and Cleveland.[34]

The arrest and death of prominent Galveston gangsters after a blazing gunbattle on Tremont Street in 1931 left the business without leadership. This was an opportunity for Sam and Rosario (Rose) Maceo, brothers who had moved to Galveston from Louisiana to set up barbershops shortly before World War I. They drifted into smuggling wine in the 1920s and in the 1930s took over illegal drinking and gambling on the island and nearby mainland. For the Maceo brothers gaming was most important and in 1926 they opened the Hollywood Dinner Club for drinking,

Phil Harris, a big band leader, gave a free concert from Murdoch's Bathhouse to 12,000 fans seated along the seawall in August 1939. *Photograph courtesy the Rosenberg Library, Galveston, Texas.*

dancing, and gambling. Affable Sam, a flower in his lapel, greeted customers while brusque Rose stayed in the back rooms and kept track of the accounts. They opened the Turf Club for gambling on horse races in downtown Galveston, and rented out pinball, phonograph, and slot machines to the small merchants of the town.

The Maceos' most impressive venture was the establishment in 1942 of the Balinese Room, a nightclub on a two-hundred-foot pier reaching into the Gulf off the seawall. Here patrons could have cocktails, eat dinner, dance to big-name bands, and spend money at the gaming tables. Liquor by the drink remained illegal in Texas

The Balinese Room, a nightclub at the end of a pier, provided illegal drinks and gambling in the 1940s at the height of Galveston's era as a sin city. Owned by the Maceo brothers, it repeatedly avoided successful raids by the Texas Rangers. Its illegal gambling and liquor service was finally ended in 1957. There are few photographs of the inside of the casino; the picture below is taken from a postcard. *Photograph, above, courtesy David G. McComb; postcard, below, courtesy the Rosenberg Library, Galveston, Texas.*

Galveston hosted a Bathing Girl Review from 1920 to 1931. This picture of the contest winners illustrates the rapid evolution of female bathing costumes during the 1920s. *Courtesy the Rosenberg Library, Galveston, Texas.*

even after the end of Prohibition in 1933 and so did gambling. But somehow the Maceos always seemed to know about a police raid before it took place and always presented a clean appearance at their clubs. According to legend, once, when state officers charged down the pier to raid the Balinese Room, the band struck up "The Eyes of Texas," and the leader announced, "And now, ladies and gentlemen, we give you in person, the Texas Rangers!"[35]

Galveston, however, was more than gambling, drinking, and sex—although for some people this was quite enough. Yankee soldiers taught local young men how to play baseball and Galveston fielded a Texas League team fairly consistently from 1888 through 1937. Jack Johnson, the black boxing champion from 1908 to 1915, grew up on the docks of Galveston and began his career fighting for the small change offered by sporting men who wanted to see a fight between black youngsters. Surf bathing and fishing were the most popular outdoor activities throughout Galveston history. Nude swimming from the docks and beach was common for men and boys, although in 1865 the city made it illegal during daylight hours. In 1877 the city required bathing costumes that covered the body from neck to knee with the exception of arms. Toward the end of the century bathhouses appeared where people could change clothes and rent bathing suits. Bathing beauty contests started in 1920 and thus the trend toward less cloth and more skin began, which continues to the present.

Both commercial and sport fishing flourished, which meant a ready supply of oysters, shrimp, and red snapper for Galveston dining tables. Flounder, redfish, Spanish mackerel, sheepshead, croakers, and speckled trout were available for fishers of all sorts, but the most spectacular sport fish was the silver king tarpon. As large as a man, the tarpon, shimmering silver in the wet sunlight, would leap five to six feet out of the water as it tried to shake off a hook. They were a thrill to watch, and from 1938 to 1965, when it was possible to catch them from piers and jetties, Galveston held annual tarpon fishing contests.

Tolerance for religion, as well as crime, was present in Galveston and the Kempners, one of the important dynastic families, although Jewish in origin, experienced little anti-Semitism. Isaac Kempner (1873–1967), important in the founding of the commission government, commented, "Oh, I've got one child married to a Jew, one child married to a Baptist, one child married to an Episcopalian, and one child married to a Catholic, and I am president of the Synagogue."[36] Rabbi Henry Cohen (1863–1952), one of the most remarkable Jewish leaders of Texas history, worked in Galveston and stood shoulder to shoulder with the Roman Catholic Father James M. Kirwin (1872–1926) before the city commissioners in 1922 to block a parade permit for the Ku Klux Klan.[37]

Blacks, however, lived a segregated life in housing, theaters, churches, sports, restaurants, and schools. There was even a separate portion of the beach between Twenty-eighth and Twenty-ninth Streets, known as Brown Beach, which was the only Gulf recreation site for blacks in Texas. During the Reconstruction era, however, George T. Ruby (1841–1882) of Galveston emerged as a leader in Texas politics and demonstrated the capability of black politicians. Norris Wright Cuney (1846–1898), meanwhile, became a force in Galveston economic life in the 1880s when he organized a union of black dock workers, the Cotton Jammer's Association. "Negroes are human beings," he said, "and should be considered from that standpoint . . . . In their actions and manner of life, they are prompted by very much the same motives actuating others of the human family."[38] Still, segregation remained until the civil rights revolution of the 1960s.

Galveston's life as a sin city came to an end in the 1950s. Sam Maceo died of cancer in 1951 and Rose passed away from heart disease in 1953. The Internal Revenue Service, meanwhile, pursued tax evasion lawsuits against the Maceo enterprises, and in 1957 Texas Attorney General Will Wilson closed forty-seven clubs, bingo places, and brothels for openly breaking the laws of the state. Texas Rangers smashed the slot machines and dumped them in Galveston Bay. The legal action and the death of Maceo leadership ended the "Free State of Galveston." As Councilwoman Ruth Levy Kempner commented in 1962 about a possible resuscitation of gambling, "We'll obey the law. Galveston is not a place apart."[39]

In 1982 the Galveston Historical Foundation successfully completed the restoration of the iron-hulled, nineteenth-century "tall ship" *Elissa*. Volunteers maintain and sail the ship, which tourists may visit at the Texas Seaport Museum located at Pier 21 near the Strand. *Photograph courtesy the Galveston Historical Foundation.*

3.
THE TOURIST CITY

AFTER THE FALL OF THE VICE TRIAD Galveston was left with a declining port, a growing medical school (which paid no city taxes), paint-weathered Victorian houses, an abandoned downtown, intact armor against hurricanes, a magnificent beach, and good weather. Galveston was still a different sort of place, like an old lady rocking on a porch with tales to tell and a twinkle in her eye, but no longer important in the mainstream of life. The problem for the city in the second half of the twentieth century was to find a reason for being; the solution was to entice the world to stop and listen to the old woman rocking patiently on the porch.

Tourism is a much ignored phenomenon in academic studies, and tourists are a much maligned creature. In Galveston the folk statement about Houstonians was, "They come down here with a dirty T-shirt and a five dollar bill and never change either one of them." The editor of the Galveston *Daily News* commented, "The problem in Galveston is residents call all tourists by their first names—Damn!"[40] Yet, tourism had been important for Galveston. Travelers had visited the town for recreation from the time of its founding, and even the illicit traffic in drinking, gambling, and sex of the Maceo era was a kind of tourist trade. After the 1950s, however, it had to become moral and legitimate.

The sandy Gulf shore had long been an attractive natural element and Galvestonians had built tourist facilities there before

Bathhouses, such as Murdoch's, on the Gulf shore rented bathing suits and provided a place to change clothes during the first half of the twentieth century. This service cost twenty-five cents in 1913. *Photograph courtesy the Rosenberg Library, Galveston, Texas.*

the construction of the seawall—a dance pavilion (1881–1883) with the first electric lights in Texas and the Beach Hotel (1883–1898) with two hundred rooms. The seawall and jetties, however, interrupted the currents and the deposit of beach sand by the waves. In places the beach eroded right into the riprap. Near the point where Broadway reached the sea, however, the wall angled inland and sand accumulated. Here, Mayor Brantly Harris established in 1941 the first municipal beach in Texas. On land donated by real estate developer Maco Stewart Jr. (1896–1950) in memory of his father, and with monies from the Works Projects Administration and city bonds, the town built a

From 1916 to 1965 Galveston merchants sponsored "Splash Day" as the opening of the summer beach season. City officials, however, had to end the celebration because of riotous crowds. College students continue to come to Galveston on spring break. *Photograph courtesy the Rosenberg Library, Galveston, Texas.*

boardwalk, pavilion, gift shop, snack bar, roller skating rink, and bathhouse.[41]

With low prices, sand raked clean of seaweed, and lifeguards, Stewart Beach welcomed families. After the completion of the Gulf Freeway to Houston in 1952 the beach became the backyard playground for the people of Houston. During the integration movement of the early 1960s, young black students led by Kelton Sams of Galveston targeted Stewart Beach along with Walgreens, Dairy Queen, and other stores. With some anxiousness but no violence the Galveston segregation barriers crumbled under the pressure. When the Killeen Chamber of Commerce wrote to the Stewart Beach Board of Managers in 1962 about a visit of the Killeen High School band, which had two black members, the beach board replied that the beach was open to all people regardless of race.[42] Segregation was over and it was reflected in the recreational policies.

THEN AND NOW

ASHTON VILLA

James M. Brown (1821–1895) built one of the first brick mansions in Texas in 1858–1859. Ashton Villa, as it was known, retained its original plaster work, frescoes, French panel mirrors, cast-iron grillwork, and supposedly the ghost of Miss Rebecca Brown, who still played the piano in the gold room when the house was threatened with destruction in 1968. The El Mina Shrine Temple, which owned it, wanted to sell or destroy the house. In a close race the city blocked demolition and bought the property so it could be managed by the Galveston Historical Foundation. The struggle to save the house provided a local lesson concerning the coordination of private and public interests, the importance of popular support, and the significance of historic preservation for the future of the city. Located at 2328 Broadway, Ashton Villa, which is open for tours, became a popular and successful tourist site.

Galveston also discovered the worth of old buildings as an attraction for visitors. Anne A. Brindley, who was active in the Chamber of Commerce and the Texas State Historical Association, rallied the elite of the city in 1957 to conserve the Williams-Tucker House at 3601 Avenue P. Samuel May Williams had built the home in 1839 with precut timber from Maine. It was one of the oldest on the island. The Galveston Historical Foundation (GHF) restored it and opened the house to tourists in 1959. James C. Massey of the National Park Service reinforced the idea of historic preservation in 1966 with a joint speech to the foundation, Chamber of Commerce, and City Council in which he pointed out that people traveled thousands of miles to see historic buildings. In the same year architect Howard Barnstone published a book with photographs by Henri Cartier-Bresson and Ezra Stoller, *The Galveston That Was*, which dramatized the city's nineteenth-century architectural treasures with fine black-and-white photographs.[43]

The GHF then sponsored a detailed inventory of twenty-five buildings and the result emphasized the importance of Ashton Villa, "Old Red" at the Medical School, the George Sealy House, and the Strand, which was the old business center of the city. The

Ashton Villa, located on Broadway, represents one of the early victories of the Galveston Historical Foundation to preserve Galveston historical sites. Built in the 1850s by James M. Brown, the villa is one of the first brick mansions in Texas. Open to visitors, it is one of the most popular tourist places in the city. *Photograph by David G. McComb.*

THEN AND NOW
THE BISHOP'S PALACE

Architect Nicholas J. Clayton (1840–1916), born in Ireland but educated in Cincinnati, came to Galveston to supervise the building of the First Presbyterian Church in 1872. He remained and became the most important architect of the city during the high Victorian era. Many of his creations have been destroyed, but the the Bishop's Palace and "Old Red," the first building on the medical school campus, still stand. Col. Walter Gresham (1841–1920) wanted the most elegant house in Texas and in 1886 Clayton designed for him a stone castle with four-story towers for a cramped site at Broadway and Fourteenth Street. In 1923 the Roman Catholic Diocese of Galveston bought the Gresham house as a home for Bishop Christopher E. Byrne, who marveled that he would reside in such a palace. The bishop died in 1950 and the "Bishop's Palace" opened for tours in 1963.

foundation won a nip-and-tuck demolition race to save Ashton Villa and added other historic sites such as the Grand Opera House, Customs House, Garten Verein Pavilion, the East End Historical District, and the Silk Stocking Historic Precinct. The center piece of restoration effort, however, was the Strand, known as the "Wall Street of the South." Led by Peter H. Brink, the executive director of the GHF from 1973 to 1989, the foundation took over the old iron-front business buildings with the hope that investors would restore them. Their thought was that history was not only interesting, but also profitable.

Fortunately, there existed local money to help the foundation accomplish its goals. When William L. Moody Jr. (1865–1954) of Galveston died he arranged for the bulk of his estate—some $440 million—to be placed in a trust for the benefit of health, education, science, and religion in Texas. Moody and his father had made this fortune in the cotton and insurance businesses, and he designated his daughter Mary Moody Northen (1892–1986) to direct the donations. The trust provided funds for the purchase of the first buildings of the Strand, a later restoration of the Moody Mansion,

Col. Walter Gresham wanted the most elegant home in Texas and Nicholas J. Clayton designed for him this castle with stone towers. The Roman Catholic Diocese bought the home in 1923 as a residence for Bishop Christopher E. Byrne. Thus, it became known as "The Bishop's Palace." *Photograph by David G. McComb.*

THEN AND NOW
THE MOODY MANSION

Col. William L. Moody (1828–1920) made a fortune with cotton after the Civil War. William L. Moody Jr. (1865–1954) expanded the amount of wealth with insurance, hotels, newspapers, and ranching. When he died he placed the bulk of his estate, some $440 million, in the Moody Foundation directed by his daughter, Mary Moody Northen (1892–1986). The foundation has aided Galveston's quest to create tourist attractions with donations for historic preservation and the building of Moody Gardens. The Moody Mansion at Broadway and Twenty-sixth where the family lived has been restored to its early twentieth century condition and is open for visits at regular hours. Somewhat less conspicuous is the Moody archives located behind the house. This library is a treasure trove of information about the Moody family and Galveston history.

and the building of Moody Gardens.[44] Other major actors were George P. Mitchell and his wife, Cynthia, who bought six buildings in the Strand, restored the Tremont Hotel, established a gourmet restaurant, and built the San Luis Hotel behind the seawall on the site of old Fort Crockett. The Mitchells encouraged, furthermore, the revival of Mardi Gras in 1985 and the start of "Dickens Evening on the Strand" in 1974 as celebrations to help Galveston weather its winter tourist doldrums.[45]

The most dramatic example of restoration was the rebuilding of the *Elissa*, found as a rusting iron hull in the harbor at Piraeus, Greece, where it was waiting to be cut into scrap. In its working life in the nineteenth century the ship had twice visited the docks of Galveston. It had undergone many transformations, but the Galveston Historical Foundation had it brought to Galveston, where it was painstakingly restored through the generous help of the Moody Foundation and the hundreds of volunteers who came from around South Texas to scrape, paint, and varnish. The result was a rare three-masted, square-rigged "tall ship" for Texas.[46] Berthed near the Strand, the *Elissa* evolved into more than a tourist attraction. It sailed in international celebrations, carried the

THEN AND NOW
THE ELISSA

The most dramatic restoration project in Galveston was the rebuilding of the three-masted, square-rigged, iron barque *Elissa* that had visited the port in 1883 and 1886. Peter Throckmorton, a marine archaeologist, found the iron hull of the ship in Piraeus, Greece, and in 1975 the Galveston Historical Foundation took on the *Elissa* as a project. Greek welders patched the rusted ship, and a towing vessel brought it back to Galveston for restoration. It was painstakingly rebuilt and sailed once more in 1982. It has since been maintained in sailing condition by volunteer "Jack Tars" from around South Texas. The ship can be seen and and its story can be heard at the Texas Seaport Museum, at Pier 21 near the Strand.

name of Galveston, flew the Lone Star banner from its masthead, and became a point of pride for the residents of the city.

Galveston, however, had to try restoration of a different sort to save its most important tourist asset, the beach. Due to wave action and storms, beaches commonly erode and disappear in front of a seawall. This happened in Galveston and starting in the 1930s the Army Corps of Engineers experimented with groins, slender finger-like extensions reaching into the Gulf at right angles to the wall. The thought was that they would trap sand drifting parallel to the shoreline. The groins were only partly successful in halting erosion and created dangerous currents for nearby swimmers. In 1994–1995, however, the city spent $5.9 million to dredge sand from offshore to rebuild the beach for the enjoyment of its six million visitors per year. This was at a cost of about one dollar per tourist if it lasted for just a year, less if it endured, and tourism could pay for it. In 1970 Galveston was the first city in Texas to adopt a tourist tax for hotel rooms so the idea of tapping tourist spending to support city facilities was not new. Alas, in September 1998 Tropical Storm Frances sent waves over the seawall, flooded the Strand knee deep with seawater, and washed away the beach. The city manager reported that the shore had lost three vertical

THEN AND NOW

THE ROSENBERG LIBRARY

Henry Rosenberg (1824–1893), born in Switzerland, arrived in Galveston at age nineteen and proceeded to make a fortune in dry goods and banking. At his death he gave $400,000 to establish a public library, and the new library opened in 1904 at 2310 Sealy Avenue. Frank C. Patten, who was the first director (from 1904 to 1934), was a bit of a pack rat and thus collected maps, manuscripts, business ledgers, artifacts, and letters. Collecting continued after Patten's era with the result that today the Rosenberg Library possesses one of the best local urban archives in Texas and the Southwest. Genealogists and historians alike use the resources of the third-floor reserve collections, and the library serves as a reservoir of information for the city's historic preservation efforts.

feet of sand. It would have to be rebuilt and continually renourished, but it was worth it for the tourist trade, Galveston's main source of revenue.[47]

Tourism brought some other interesting problems when the numbers of visitors went beyond the resources of the city. Splash Day, a celebration of the opening to the swimming season in April, began in 1916 but had to be halted in 1965 because the police could not keep law and order in the huge crowds. More recently the city has been overwhelmed by the spring "beach bash" of Kappa Alpha Psi, a national black college fraternity. The bash mushroomed yearly in numbers since it began in 1983 as more and more outsiders arrived to hear the beach concerts and crash the dances. Mostly young revelers, up to 150,000 in number, jammed the fast food places and their toilets. In 1997 traffic on the Gulf Freeway halted with a twelve-mile, two-hour traffic gridlock. In 1998 the city spent an extra $200,000 on portable toilets and policemen. In 1999, with visitors nearing 200,000, the traffic jammed and a man stuck on Interstate 45 simply set up his barbecue equipment on the roadway and started to cook. For Galveston it was too much tourism. As Park Board Director

Wendy Dehnert said, "It's basically something that's been forced on us."[48]

The "Kappa" difficulty and the problems of beach sand, however, were only glitches in the overall success of Galveston as a tourist city. The town survived the worst natural catastrophe in the history of the nation, it lived through a period of illegal gambling and wide-open prostitution, it changed itself into a family recreation destination. Galveston at the start of the new millennium offered to the traveler a chance to enjoy warm breezes, pastel-colored sunsets, interesting seafood, glimpses of history, and a chance to meditate while feeling nature's pulsebeat of waves in the shallow surf. Compared to the compulsive economic obsession of the great Texas metropolises, Galveston indeed, was a different place.

The beach with its warmth, water, and sunshine has been a constant interest for visitors from the beginning of Galveston's history. These five young women of the early 1920s seated on the riprap in front of the seawall with their parasols illustrate this attraction. *Photograph courtesy the Rosenberg Library, Galveston, Texas.*

NOTES

1. Charles W. Hays, *Galveston: A History of the Island and the City* (2 vols.; Austin: Jenkins Garrett, 1974), I, 170–180, II, 811–814. David G. McComb, *Galveston, a History* (Austin: University of Texas Press, 1986), 42–43.

2. Galveston *Daily News*, June 28, 1891.

3. Francis C. Sheridan, *Galveston Island; or, a Few Months Off the Coast of Texas: The Journal of Francis C. Sheridan, 1839–1840*, ed. Willis W. Pratt (Austin: University of Texas Press, 1954), 32 (1st quotation), 53 (2nd quotation).

4. M. C. Houstoun, *Texas and the Gulf of Mexico; or, Yachting in the New World* (London: John Murray, 1844), 275.

5. McComb, *Galveston*, 12–23.

6. W. W. Newcomb Jr., *The Indians of Texas* (Austin: University of Texas Press,1961), 63–81. See also Robert A. Ricklis, *The Karankawa Indians of Texas* (Austin: University of Texas Press, 1996).

7. Robert S. Weddle, *Spanish Sea: The Gulf of Mexico in North American Discovery, 1500–1685* (College Station: Texas A&M University Press, 1985), 185–197.

8. Cyclone Covey, *Cabeza de Vaca's Adventures in the Unknown Interior of America* (New York: Collier Books, 1961), 55–60, 124–128.

9. W. B., "Life of Jean Laffite," *Littell's Living Age*, 32 (Mar. 6,

1852), 441. T., "The Cruise of the Enterprise," *United States Magazine and Democratic Review*, 6 (July, 1839), 38–42.

10. Hays, *Galveston*, I, 260–262, II, 815.

11. Sheridan, *Galveston Island*, 37.

12. McComb, *Galveston*, 45–47.

13. Ibid., 56.

14. Ibid., 50–51.

15. Ibid., 59–61.

16. Ibid., 150. See also Marilyn McAdams Sibley, *The Port of Houston: A History* (Austin: University of Texas Press, 1968); David G. McComb, *Houston, a History* (Austin: University of Texas Press, 1981), 65–70; and current issues of the *Texas Almanac* (Dallas: Dallas *Morning News*) for port statistics.

17. David G. McComb, "Galveston as a Tourist City," *Southwestern Historical Quarterly*, 100 (Jan., 1997), 335.

18. Dora Fowler Arthur, "Jottings from the Old Journal of Littleton Fowler," *Quarterly of the Texas State Historical Association*, 2 (July, 1898), 82.

19. Joe B. Frantz, *Gail Borden: Dairyman to a Nation* (Norman: University of Oklahoma Press, 1951), 129, 152–159, 173, 176, 198, 203–220.

20. Ralph A. Wooster, *Civil War Texas: A History and a Guide* (Austin: Texas State Historical Association, 1999), 15–20.

21. Anne Lois Moore Buckhorn, "The Yellow Fever Epidemic of 1867 in Galveston" (M.A. thesis, University of Houston, 1962), 43, 47, 52, 126; McComb, *Galveston*, 92–97.

22. *The University of Texas Medical Branch at Galveston: A Seventy-five Year History by the Faculty and Staff* (Austin: University of Texas Press, 1967), 15–19, 23.

23. Brownson Malsch, *Indianola: The Mother of Western Texas* (Austin: Shoal Creek, 1977), 236–244, 253–254. Galveston *Daily News*, May 11, 1894; Sept. 11, 1895.

24. Erik Larson, *Isaac's Storm* (New York: Crown, 1999) blames the weather service and Cline for lack of proper warning, but even

Cline's house and family were swept away by the hurricane.

25. McComb, *Galveston*, 121–134. See also Clarence Ousley (ed.), *Galveston in Nineteen Hundred* (Atlanta: Chase, 1900); Joseph L. Cline, *When the Heavens Frowned* (Dallas: Mathis, Van Nort, 1946); Isaac M. Cline, *Storms, Floods and Sunshine* (New Orleans: Pelican, 1945); John Edward Weems, *A Weekend in September* (College Station: Texas A&M University Press, 1957); Elizabeth Hayes Turner and Patricia Bellis Bixel, *Catastrophe and Catalyst: Galveston, Texas and the 1900 Hurricane* (Austin: University of Texas Press, forthcoming); Shelly Henly Kelly and Casey Edward Greene, *Voices from the Storm* (College Station: Texas A&M University Press, forthcoming).

26. Bradley Robert Rice, *Progressive Cities: The Commission Government Movement in America, 1901–1920* (Austin: University of Texas Press, 1977), 7–16. McComb, *Galveston*, 134–137. The myth that the business elite heroically created the commission government in order to save Galveston from an inept city government is followed by Harold M. Hyman in *Oleander Odyssey: The Kempners of Galveston, Texas, 1854–1980s* (College Station: Texas A&M University Press, 1990), 145–153.

27. Galveston *Daily News*, Aug. 8, 1909.

28. Albert B. Davis, *Galveston's Bulwark Against the Sea: History of the Galveston Seawall* (Galveston: U.S. Army Engineering District, 1961), 5, 11–14, 18–19; McComb, *Galveston*, 138–140.

29. McComb, *Galveston*, 142–143.

30. Galveston *Daily News*, May 25, 26, 1912.

31. Galveston *Daily News*, Aug. 18–23, 25, Sept. 12, 1915.

32. *Texas Almanac, 1992–1993*, 172.

33. For comparison, the ratio of prostitutes to citizens in Paris in 1934 was 1:481. A general discussion of the red-light district can be found in McComb, *Galveston*, 155–158, but an extraordinary inside look was provided in 1930 by Granville Price, who wrote a master's thesis about the district for the University of Texas, "A Sociological Study of a Segregated District."

34. Galveston *Daily News*, Dec. 11, 1930.

35. Jack Lait and Lee Mortimer, *USA Confidential* (New York: Crown, 1952), 215–217; Alan Walman, "Big Sam and Papa Rose," *InBetween*, 55 (Aug., 1979), 29, 47; McComb, *Galveston*, 161–166, 175–178.

36. Galveston *Daily News*, July 27, 1969; Harris L. Kempner to Robert L. Jones, June 17, 18, 1980, interview, transcript, p. 19 (Oral History Collection, Rosenberg Library, Galveston).

37. See A. Stanley Dreyfus, *Henry Cohen, Messenger of the Lord* (New York: Block, 1963), 20, 41–42, 57, 59, 73.

38. Maud Cuney Hare, *Norris Wright Cuney: A Tribune of the Black People* (Austin: Steck-Vaughn, 1968), 31.

39. Galveston *Daily News*, Aug. 1, 1962; McComb, *Galveston*, 184–187.

40. Quoted by Terri A. Castaneda, "Preservation and the Cultural Politics of the Past on Historic Galveston Island" (Ph.D. diss., Rice University, 1993), 81–82.

41. McComb, "Galveston as a Tourist City," 353.

42. Galveston *Daily News*, July 7, 8, 15, 1960; Minutes of the Board of Managers, Stewart Beach, May 12, 1962 (Rosenberg Library, Galveston).

43. Galveston *Daily News*, June 2, 1966; Howard Barnstone, *The Galveston That Was* (New York: Macmillan, 1966).

44. Galveston *Daily News*, Apr. 27, 1973; McComb, "Galveston as a Tourist City," 358. See also Gary Cartwright, *Galveston, a History of the Island* (New York: Atheneum, 1991) for a lucid account of the family infighting involved for control of the foundation.

45. McComb, "Galveston as a Tourist City," 358–359.

46. Ibid., 359.

47. Galveston *Daily News*, Sept. 11–13, 1998; McComb, "Galveston as a Tourist City," 359–360.

48. Galveston *Daily News*, Apr. 17, 19, 20 [quotation], 22 ,1997; Apr. 19, 1998; Apr. 18, 1999.

INDEX

David G. McComb grew up in Houston, Texas, and is now a professor of history at Colorado State University in Fort Collins, Colorado. He is a fellow of the Texas State Historical Association and has written five books about Texas, including *Houston, a History* (1981), *Galveston, a History* (1989), *Texas, a Modern History* (1989), and *The Historic Seacoast of Texas* (1999) with J. U. Salvant. At the present he is studying the development of coastal cities and the impact of tourism.